ASPIRE TO INSPIRE

For every woman who pauses, then performs

AF491722

DANIYAH IRFAN

INDIA • SINGAPORE • MALAYSIA

FROM THE AUTHOR'S DESK

With every word I write and share,
Planting a dream, a hope, a dare,
To touch the hearts & ignite the fire,
The mission is clear: Aspire to Inspire.

Before you dive into these pages, I want to extend my heartfelt thanks for picking up this book. You're about to embark on a journey that is as much about self-discovery as it is about empowerment, and I am thrilled to have you along for the ride.

Think of this book as your personal roadmap through the paths of career comebacks and personal growth—complete with all the bumps and detours I faced, so you can navigate them with a bit more grace and ease. As a nutritionist with a deep passion for guiding women on their health, i also mentor you for career paths after your break, I am honoured to be your steadfast coach on this journey.

Aspire to Inspire is a collection of my most genuine and transformative experiences. Each chapter is filled with lessons I learned , delivered with the hope that my insights can spark a difference in your life. Writing to me was a natural extension of my love for expressing in solitude and observing that many of my quirkiest reflections came to me in the quiet moments, lying in bed, awaiting the narration to unfold through the book.

Welcome to what I like to call your "second innings"—a chance where dreams are not just chased but actually captured and lived. Together, we will laugh through the setbacks and celebrate the victories.

As the saying goes, *"Life isn't about waiting for the storm to pass, but learning to dance in the rain." Let's dance through the challenges and embrace the opportunities that lie ahead!

Thank you again for joining me on this adventure. Let's get started!.

DEDICATION

All my work in the book is dedicated to my mother. Grateful to you for instilling in me undying spirit and resilience to face challenges. Love you.

All of a sudden, I feel euphoric and also feeling like melting down emotionally as I bow down in gratitude to the creator of this universe.

CONTENTS

ACKNOWLEDGEMENTS

It's a blessing to have loving daughters, spouse and supportive friends and colleagues who always kept me motivated and compelled me to finish writing this book. The immense love I convey to my siblings, this would never have been possible without their support.

I'm ever grateful to all my mentors whom I met on my way— Mr Arfeen Khan, who guided me into life coaching; Dr Suresh Kumar, who is my backbone support towards learning holistic nutrition and Dr Vishal Marwah, with whom I learned the nuances of entrepreneurship.

The first thing that I learned from them was that *change begins with a change within*, which helped me emerge from my shackles of negative self-talk and low self-image.

This book would not have been published if it were not for a quest for inspiration I want to sow in the minds of many women across the globe.

THE WRITE WAY: MY SECOND INNINGS JOURNEY

Two days before the big event, I was a whirlwind of nerves and excitement, pacing my house like a caged tiger. Every few minutes, I'd glance at my reflection in the mirror, practising my opening line with the conviction of a TED talk speaker. The frenzy was real. I Googled "how to conquer stage fright" so many times that even my search engine started suggesting breathing exercises and motivational quotes. My fridge was a battlefield of sticky notes, each bearing a word of encouragement or a reminder to breathe—because apparently, in my nervous state, I'd forget. I tried to distract myself with yoga but ended up tangled. I attempted to bake cookies to calm my mind, but instead of a batch of delicious treats, I ended up with something resembling charred hockey pucks.

By the eve of the event, my house looked like a self-help seminar had exploded inside it. Pep talks played on a loop while I practised my speech, and my youngest girl watched with a mixture of pity and amusement. I was a bundle of jittery energy, ready to combust at any moment.

And then, the day arrived. In the hustle and bustle of the city, where taxis honked like an orchestra of impatient drivers and the weather couldn't decide between a drizzle and a downpour, I found myself standing backstage, heart pounding against my ribs like a drum solo at a rock concert. The relentless beat of my anxiety matched the frenetic pace of the city outside.

Gripping the microphone, I felt the weight of expectation pressing down on me. The fear of stumbling over my words, of becoming a viral sensation for all the wrong reasons, of becoming a walking disaster, threatened to swallow me whole.

But then, as I started to speak, something miraculous happened. Instead of the anticipated chaos, a strange sense of calm washed over me. Though my knees still knocked like they were auditioning for a tap dance, my voice found its rhythm, weaving through the silence with a newfound confidence.

As I spoke, the crowd before me blurred into a sea of indistinct faces, their murmurs melting into the background like the city's white noise. All that mattered was the connection forged in that moment, my raw vulnerability laid bare for all to see.

And then, amidst the thunderous applause that reverberated through the room like a busy train passing by, she appeared—a lone figure in the ocean of faces. Her words cut through the noise like fresh hope....

"Daniyah, you have just inspired me," she said, her voice a gentle whisper amidst the roaring approval. In that instant, I realised the true power of the ability to connect, to uplift and maybe, just maybe, to make someone feel a little less alone.

Who knew baring your soul could be this exhilarating? Or that public speaking could transform from a dreaded nightmare into a moment of triumph? If you're curious about how to turn your own inhibitions into inspiring stories, buckle up—this book is your guide to turning those heart-pounding moments into unforgettable successes.

And remember, if I can navigate through the whirlwind of my own nerves and insecurities, so can you.

This is not just a story of triumph over fear. It is a reminder that even in our moments of greatest vulnerability, we have the power to inspire, to uplift and to change the world. And so, with trembling hands and a heart full of hope, I invite you to join me on this journey—a journey of courage, of connection and of the endless possibilities that lie within each of us.

I learned one thing that day by sharing my story and vulnerabilities, that humans connect. *So, let your story inspire the world. You never know who can be impacted by you. Just when we think we're no good, there's someone out there aspiring to live our life.*

I wasn't even into coaching then, but I was happy that I touched a life that day—how much of a 'goosebumpy' feeling did it give you? My life before this event was a normal, ordinary life, but with an extraordinary burning desire to change lives and create an impact on people's health. Just that I lacked direction and mentorship.

I'm sure you'll agree with me 100% that when we lead our lives without a goal or a purpose, life will put us through an examination of grit and resilience. In some circumstances, you will feel you are buried, in the dark with all adversities, alone and fighting your insecurities—here's when you make a choice: to stay buried and die or find the ray of light and start to bloom, making the world around you beautiful with your presence.

So, the catch here is that what choices you make create your reality of life today. Communicate with yourself, befriend yourself, spend quality time with yourself and *become a cup full of love* so that you can be the owner of your life and inspire, guide and coach others to take charge—of their life, relationships, health and wealth.

The buried seed story inspired me.

"For every door that's been opened to me, I've tried to open my door to others. And here is what I have to say, finally: Let's invite one another in. Maybe then we can begin to fear less, make fewer wrong assumptions and let go of the biases and stereotypes that unnecessarily divide us. Maybe we can better embrace the ways we are the same. It's not about being perfect. It's not about where you get yourself in the end. There's power in allowing yourself to be known and heard, owning your unique story and using your authentic voice. And there's grace in being willing to know and

hear others. This, for me, is how we become." — **Michelle Obama, Becoming.**

Today I stand proud as an author and coach. I love the attention, I simply adore the popularity it's giving me and of course, a part of me is internally beaming with pride.

Winning is not about achieving things; It is about who we become in the process of achieving them.

This is what you get as a visible reward for your hard work and mission accomplishment. What I see deeper is that today, what I am is because of how I led my life, my shortcomings, my challenges, my insecurities and my weak repertoire. This is what has made me into what I am today. Because constantly in my mind, I had fought a battle—with what my heart wanted and created a wave of transformation into a beautifully confident and strong person.

You may wonder how these qualities have etched me and brought me this far. *What you focus on more—grows more.* I chose to give more power to my strengths, capabilities and passion for people. For you to know yourself, you will need to know and accept yourself first. Know that there's nothing impossible to achieve and understand that what you seek is already there, just go and get it. How else do you think some women became great leaders in spite of challenges and hurdles? They didn't give up. They had a vision and mission in mind; they imagined themselves as successful even before they were.

As you read and learn from this book, I wish you immense luck, power, success and an improvised version of yourself. Keeping yourself in tune with yourself and gaining knowledge, upskilling, transforming, and making wonders happen is no big deal for us as women if we only keep doing our best and spreading the power of love and energy—for ourselves and for the people around us.

PREFACE

In the shadows deep, where dreams once lay,
Amidst the silence of yesterday,
Rises a phoenix, bold and bright,
A soul reborn in the softest light.

From ashes cold, where hopes had died,
Springs forth a strength that will not hide,
With wings of fire and heart of gold,
A story of life reclaimed, retold.

Through trials, dark and battles long,
Emerges a spirit, fierce and strong,
Each scar a tale of courage earned,
Each step a path where wisdom's learned.

In the dance of dawn and twilight's grace,
She finds her rhythm, her rightful place,
No longer bound by fears once named,
A life reclaimed, unchained, untamed.

With every breath, a promise kept,
In every heartbeat, dreams are swept,
A journey forward, brave and free,
A testament to what can be.

So rise again, with eyes aflame,
Embrace the world, and stake your claim,
For life reclaimed is life anew,
A brilliant sky of endless blue.

Twenty years ago, I made a decision that would change the course of my life forever. Little did I know then that this choice would eventually lead me to author a book aimed at inspiring women like me. As I write these words, I am filled with a sense of purpose and urgency. This book is not just a collection of stories; it is a call to action, a hope for women who feel trapped by their circumstances.

Life has a way of throwing unexpected challenges our way. As women, we often find ourselves at the crossroads of nurturing our families and pursuing our dreams. Many of us have faced the harsh reality of sacrificing our careers to knit together the fabric of our families. It's a role we are designed for—providing love, comfort and support. But what happens when we somehow lose ourselves in the process?

In my journey, I have encountered countless women who are unhappy, frustrated and lacking the confidence to reclaim their lives. Their stories are etched into my heart, each one a testament to the silent struggles that many women endure. I have seen women who, despite having supportive spouses and families, still find themselves unable to pursue their passions due to a lack of confidence or societal pressure. The belief that women are not meant to venture out into the "big bad world" can be a crippling shackle.

The truth is, you don't need to be employed full-time or earn a fortune to feel fulfilled. Sometimes, all it takes is engaging in small passions, those little things that light up your soul. Many women find joy in social service, while others create home-based businesses that bring them satisfaction. The essence of fulfilment lies in doing what makes you feel good and gives you a sense of purpose. This is what defines your identity and helps you reclaim your sense of self.

My journey began to alternate with one part of me being a homemaker achiever while one part of me felt a void. Internally, the second half was screaming to be released and finding that missing piece of the jigsaw that would fit in perfectly to complete my life. It was not an easy one. Taking a break years ago from my profession was like stepping into emptiness.

The years that followed were filled with moments of satisfaction as I built my family. Hand in hand was my self-doubt and the daunting task of redefining my purpose. But it was in these moments of introspection that I found the motivation to rise again. I realised that achieving the recognition and importance I deserved was not just a desire but a necessity.

Many women believe that once they leave their careers, there is no turning back. They carry the weight of societal expectations and personal inhibitions, convinced that they lack the skills or motivation to make a comeback. This book is my answer to those doubts. It is a proof to the 43% of women who leave their jobs to embrace motherhood and the myriad of reasons why they should not feel bound by that choice.

Through the pages of this book, I want to convey a powerful message: you are unstoppable. No matter how long your hiatus, no matter how deep your doubts, there is always a way to reclaim your life and your dreams. This book is filled with stories of women who have done just that—each one a ray of hope that endorses the resilience of the female spirit.

The title of this book was chosen with great care. It encapsulates my mission: to inspire, to motivate and to unleash the potential within every woman who reads it. So, as you turn the pages, I invite you to experience this journey with me. Together, we will explore the stories of women who have risen from the ashes, who have embraced their passions, and who have become unstoppable forces.

This is just a movement towards self-discovery, empowerment and the relentless pursuit of dreams. Read on, and discover the ways to unleash yourself and become limitless, no matter the obstacles you have faced. This is your time, your journey and your story.

INTRODUCTION

wo defining moments that were a breakthrough and made me push myself were my mum's aspiration for me to make it big in my profession, for which she would unload maximum ideas, and my better half, who kept me on my mission always.

When you are setting out to make changes and you have a deep desire to transform, try looking within. Many times, with life's demands, people's pressure and our own expectations of ourselves, we are in a state of inner conflict. Sometimes, we do not know whether anything that we are doing will satisfy us or if it is so important that it can take away all the sanity that we deserve.

In a fast-paced town lived a woman named Aanya—a fantastic and fun girl but also as fragile as a porcelain teacup. On the outside, Aanya's life seemed perfect. She had a loving family, a comfortable home and a stable routine that would make even the most disciplined monk envious. But beneath this polished life, she was crumbling.

Aanya often confided in me, revealing the brittle state of her inner self. "90% of my time is devoted to everyone else," she would say, her voice tinged with exhaustion and just a hint of sarcasm. "I don't even know what I like to eat or what clothes I prefer to wear." Her eyes would well up with tears, reflecting a deep sense of loss and confusion.

Her identity crisis peaked at her wedding when her name was changed. "How unfair is that?" she exclaimed one day, her frustration palpable. "You are being forced to be called something of which you have no identity!" It was as if she had suddenly been cast in a play where she didn't even get to choose her character's name.

As the years passed, Aanya's sense of self continued to erode. She moved through life like a shadow, her own desires and needs buried under the weight of her responsibilities. Her days were spent juggling everything from PTA meetings to making Pinterest-worthy birthday cakes, leaving no room for her own whims and fancies.

One day, Aanya stood in front of her wardrobe, staring blankly at the sea of beige cardigans and practical shoes. "Who am I?" she muttered, half expecting a Disney fairy godmother to pop out and tell her. But alas, no magical intervention came.

Instead, she decided to take a step—a small one—towards rediscovering herself. One afternoon, as we sat in her garden, she opened up about her deepest fears. "I don't even recognise myself anymore," she whispered, her voice breaking. "I feel invisible, like I've disappeared." Her vulnerability was heartbreaking.

Together, we embarked on a journey of self-discovery. We started small—exploring her favourite foods, finding clothes that made her feel confident, and carving out time for activities she enjoyed. Slowly, she began to reconnect with herself and joined her community social service centre. She found her purpose.

She also bought a bright red dress, the kind that screamed confidence. As she twirled in front of the mirror, a small smile crept onto her face. Maybe, just maybe, Aanya was starting to find the person she once knew herself to be, one colourful dress at a time. And while her journey was just beginning, it was clear that this fun, fantastic and slightly frazzled woman was ready to reclaim her identity with a touch of humour and a lot of heart.

Over time, Aanya's brittle exterior started to heal. She learned to voice her needs and set boundaries. She accepted and healed with love, finding her lost self after so many years. Now she says, "What's in a name?" and laughs it out. God bless this beautiful soul. It does take courage to unlearn our patterns and relearn to live in joy.

Section 1

Default

DEFAULT

**'You have 2 choices; to control your mind or
let the mind control you'**

– P. Coelho

In a world where women often find themselves balancing the demands of fitness, money and relationships, it is easy to lose sight of our own internal passions and goals. The adventure of life can sometimes feel like walking on a tightrope, where one misstep may unravel the delicate balance we strive to maintain. When the mind is the master, life is often led in default mode, characterised by habitual patterns, automatic reactions, unconscious decision-making, lack of self-awareness and fluctuating emotions.

In essence, when the mind governs unchecked, default living can obscure the richness of conscious experience and the transformative power of intentional living. Recognising this dynamic invites exploration and cultivation of mindfulness, enabling individuals to transcend automaticity and embrace a more purposeful and fulfilled existence.

Here's your chance to witness the power of holistic living where our personal dreams and passions are not just acknowledged but celebrated. It is an invitation to every woman to reclaim her narrative, to change her life from default to design that is rich with purpose and joy.

We need to do a better job of keeping ourselves higher on our own to-do list.

By embracing a balanced existence, you not only enhance your own experience but also inspire those around you. Together, we can create a ripple effect of positive change, proving that it is possible to live fully and passionately while taking care of all that matters. This is your time to shine.

In the journey of life, women with flaws create the most inspiring stories. They face struggles and setbacks, but they always find a way to rise up, driven by their own inner strength. Embracing their imperfections, they turn challenges into opportunities for growth. These women show us that true power comes from resilience and determination.

In the following chapters, I bring to you 6 types of women (on the basis of my observation) whose minds are keeping them anchored in a *zone of no progress*. It's interesting to find out who and how!

 # 1. MADAM PAST TENSE

In shadows of the past dwells Madam Past Tense,
Caught in a never-ending spell, life feels so dense,
Old wounds and dreams left unfulfilled,
Her spirit dampened and hopes quietly stilled.
Prisoner of memories, she remains,
Regrets and sorrows, endless chains,
Blaming life for every scar,
Seeing failures, never far.
Each regret, a heavy stone,
Her past a fortress, cold as bone,
Opportunities lost in time,
A bright future, hard to climb.
Self-doubt and blame, her daily bread,
Potential shrouded, dreams left dead,
Yet in her heart, a spark still gleams,
Awaiting dawn, awakening dreams.

Look around you, and you'll find a woman who is always looking for an excuse to blame people and situations that have put her in what she's facing in the present. Such people suffer from the 'Past 'Baggage Syndrome,' unable to accept that if she's in a situation, it's because of her low energy vibration soaked in sadness or guilt.

She is always unhappy with the present, resentful and unaware that she's stuck, messing up and ruining her life. Her past experiences are so emotionally charged that 'they're not helping her make decisions in the present for a better future.

Why do you think we are living this life? Why are we bestowed with night and day or different seasons? It's so that we experience every bit, learn, gather and live our life to the fullest. Why, then, do we love to stay in the past? A part of our lives that has already passed and is not meant to be in the future. But if we keep doing the same actions, we are putting ourselves in the loop of the same results.

Every single minute is a blessing to be taken and converted into the way we want. Your mind will do as you command. It is like the genie from the lamp: "Your wish is my command." So, if your mental commands are too negative and intimidating for the mind, it will give you a similar result. Always be aware of your thoughts because these thoughts become our feelings and then our habits. Once the habit develops of pessimism and low self-talk, your reality will be inevitable. **Ask and it's given**. This holds true for any of the thoughts that we are thinking.

Now, go back and think of how many times you have thought negatively in your past, told yourself in your mind that you are good for nothing, or made decisions out of spite.

A client I came across was a 27-year-old who despised her parents' decisions. **Why?** Because they made her do things in the past which didn't go well with her and led to arguments and physical altercations with suicidal tendencies. That thought went into her subconscious so much that today, even though they are making amends for what has gone by, she's mistrusting and defensive of her decisions. Such people haven't taken the courage to understand and accept life. They are so constantly engaged in negative self-talk that their future is at stake. Every aspect of her life's decision is based on the sour experiences of the past.

What's happening here is like carrying baggage full of rotten cabbage, foul and regressive, not realising how much harm it's doing to her. She just has to try to let go of the cabbages to lead a happy and secure future. The way we deal with situations sometimes overrides sanity. We are in a rush to judge and make decisions which can be harmful in the long run.

Women! Please come out of this rut. Be aware of your own wants and feelings. If you're doing things that you don't believe in, you're in for a confused and jittery mind that's always on the lookout for a blame game. The past is gone, but we can change ourselves in the present and make the future beautiful. The hard truth is that if nothing changes around you, that means you haven't changed yourself enough. Unless you want to seek attention with pity or take revenge for the misdoings, and this drives you to live your life, nothing can be of help.

Mrs. Past Tense, life unfolds in moments that slip away into memories, but dwelling in them only binds you. Embrace each new day as a canvas for your choices, not a shadow of regrets. Let the past be a guide, not a cage. Your future awaits the joy you create today.

Help Yourself

"The solution to every problem is directly proportional to the distance between your pen and paper."

Make a note that every single day, you will write down the people you want to forgive in your life. Do not resist, don't feel it's unimportant, don't doubt or have second thoughts. It could be close people whom we deal with on a daily basis, like parents, spouses or children. It could be distant relatives or friends whom you meet sometimes, but they transfer their negative energy and impact our lives.

It could also be people whom you have met once in your lifetime who may have made a difference in your life.

❖ Make a list of people.

❖ Reflect on how they have made you feel.

❖ Against every person's name, write down your forgiveness.

❖ Keep doing it for a week; it will help you feel light.

❖ The more you express, the faster you'll get over it.

❖ Repeat every night before sleeping.

 # 2. MRS MERRY LATER

Mrs. Merry Later, dreams deferred,
In fields of time, her voice unheard,
She dances with tomorrow's song,
Procrastination's hold, so strong.

Plans and hopes, in shadows cast,
Moments fleeting, slipping fast,
Promises of "soon" and "later,"
A future bright but always greater.

Her days are filled with endless ache
Yet nights are void of realised dream.
In waiting, her potential fades,
Lost in the maze of endless trades.

But deep within, a spark still gleams,
A life beyond delayed routines,
If only she could seize today,
Mrs. Merry Later might find her way.

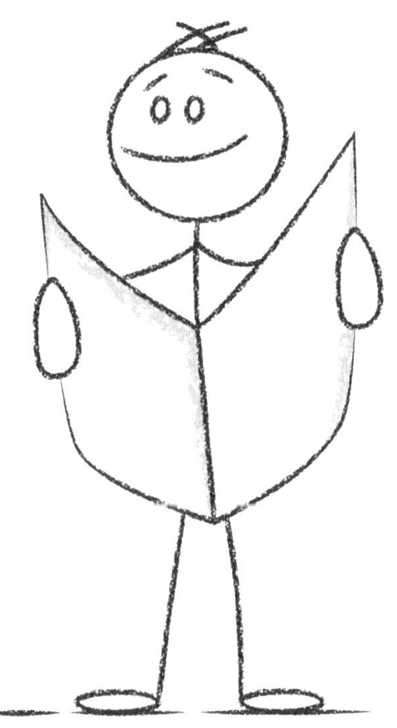

A term that we call the procrastination syndrome is so very inevitably visible in today's day and age. Be it a man, woman, child or teen—everyone is up to the brim with something to preoccupy them.

You, who are reading this book, haven't you squeezed out the time from your schedule to learn something from here that will help you in your personal or professional life?

Women today have hammered and nailed themselves into trying to fit in everywhere perfectly without listing out priorities for themselves. As working from home remotely is grabbing most of their work hours, a lot of other tasks get left out, which when not attended to on demand, gets procrastinated. Similarly, for women who have taken a break from their careers, it becomes a bigger mountain to move as there's a big lack of confidence and roadblocks that everything will take time and more skills to get back into the same career or to find a passion and work towards it to build an identity.

While I was on my hiatus and felt the urge to bounce back, after almost a couple of decades, my inner voice was the massive monster that I was facing all the time. I felt as though all of a sudden, I was faced with a big examination—of understanding myself. I thought I wasn't skilled enough, that I lacked the expertise, that my kids would be left to fend for themselves, that I would not be the same person (and, of course, you won't be) who had all 24 hours for the family. I fought, I resisted, but I understood my needs. I needed to help people, I needed to create a transformation for myself and others. **And believe me, what you seek will seek you,** eventually. After a long time spent in speculation, I stepped out and did some things that changed me slowly but steadily. I gave time to myself, for myself and enjoyed myself. There's no bigger happiness—prioritise yourself.

'If only one glass is full, can one give away something to others?'

Who can give anything to others if their own glass is empty?

That's what I realised—the happiness I experienced became a source of happiness for others. So go there, find time for yourself, don't procrastinate. Seize the day and live life enjoying the present moments.

Mrs. Merry Later, amidst everything, hear this: within you, a spark still shines. The journey to reclaiming your dreams begins with prioritising yourself. Your story is still unfolding, and with courage and determination, you can navigate towards a future where your potential is ready to unfold.

Help yourself

> ### *"The key is not to prioritise what's on your schedule, but to schedule your priorities."*

- ❖ Sit with yourself.
- ❖ List out the negative beliefs you have created for yourself.
- ❖ If they're not helping you, write them in bold.
- ❖ Look at them.
- ❖ They have been a part of you till now.
- ❖ Tear the paper or burn the paper.
- ❖ Now they're no longer a part of you.
- ❖ You have evolved.
- ❖ Repeat if required.

# 3. TIME-LESS MUMMY

In the morning's hush, children wake,
Tasks beckon, a list to make.
With a steady heart and weary sigh,
A mother starts her daily stride.

From dawn till dusk, time swiftly flies,
Chores and cares beneath the skies.
Dreams deferred, yet love prevails,
In every task, her heart unveils.

Amidst the rush, she seeks a pause,
In fleeting moments, love's applause.
For in each smile and whispered word,
A universe of love is stirred.

Haven't we all heard this very commonly - 'I don't get time for anything'...

- ❖ Do some people get more than 24 hours in a day?
- ❖ Does your TO DO list never get checked totally?
- ❖ Did you know that the concept of time means - 'the present 'moment'?
- ❖ Are you fed up with the daily routine that doesn't excite you?

A timeless mom goes through this condition called the 'I don't have the time' syndrome. I deliberately call these syndromes as they manifest cumulative features that culminate into a feeling of hopelessness. Be it, teenage girls, working women or homemakers. Why do they have this ability to never find time?

Most of the time, we do not know what we are doing with our time and why we are doing certain things. We focus all our energies on making work a drudgery instead of making it a pleasure. Most of us live to work.

How do you make a start to your day, a day that has a fresh stock of 24 hours? Wake up with an energy that your brain cells are excited to help you do something exciting. Start off the day early with a fitness regime or meditation or a spiritual ritual or connect with nature at sunrise and observe the vast span of colours it displays.

Be like the sun - that shines each day, gives life to living beings, regulates night and day and goes off to let the moon have its turn of duties to perform. What if one day the sun was bored of shining... 'same duties every day... Let me just not come up. I'll take an off day",' it thought, and decided not to rise. The next day when it rose, there was no world where it could shine.

How are success stories created? How is it that some people have money floating around and others struggle to make ends meet? Isn't it about the passion with which they plan, execute and make discoveries, too? Every invention is a product of passion... to have the courage to create something new and make life easy for others.

Prepare-Plan-Persevere is the magic mantra that overcomes resistance and welcomes change.

Help Yourself

"You don't have to see the whole staircase, just take the first step."

– Martin Luther King.

❖ Look around you.

❖ Make a note of everything you need to be thankful for.

❖ Family, friends, nature, vast universal expanse.

❖ Be grateful for everything, including the time that you get.

❖ Do gratitude meditation for 21 days and change your vibration.

 # 4. MADAM FLAWLESS

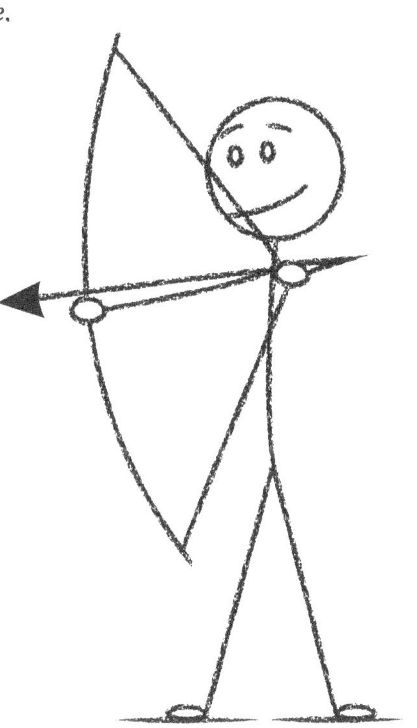

In perfect realms where shadows hide,
Lives Mrs Flawless with perfection's guide.
Each task a quest for purest form,
A struggle to outpace the norm.

Their worlds are ordered, neat, precise,
Each action planned without a vice,
No margin for a flaw or slip,
In an unyielding, iron grip.

They toil through night and day's first
light,
Adjusting, fixing, till it's right,
An endless loop of strive and mend,
Perfection's call, their only friend.

Yet in the gleam of perfect sheen,
Lies a burden, often unseen,
A heart that yearns for peace and rest,
Bound by the need to be the best.

In every spotless, gleaming floor,
A silent plea for something more,
For freedom from the ceaseless grind,
And peace within their restless mind.

Here's an uncomfortable truth about perfection: it's often just insecurity in disguise"

– Gary Vaynerchuk.

How many of you think it's a contradictory quote? That's how we were created and that's how God wants us to be - strong, happy and beautiful. Many a time, I also found myself in this circle of perfectionism. Here's what we tend to think about and take action

❖ Only once I feel I'm ready/confident/prepared will I start the practice/business.

❖ Let me do that job for her; she'll not do it well.

❖ When I'm leading a project, I want perfection - in research and presentations.

❖ Cleaning frenzy before expected guests arrive or not.

❖ No one can do it as perfectly as I do; I reach 30 minutes before schedule.

❖ A tad bit more clean and tidy.

❖ Why are people so slow?

I'm so fascinated and awestruck by the way people crave to be perfect. So much so that it becomes an obsession and they don't settle for anything less. How is it possible to be 'perfect'? It's a myth and illusion. People who seek perfection will find themselves unfulfilled their whole lives. More important is to focus on progress and the journey to achieve success instead of being perfect.

My experience as a perfectionist became very demanding for me. From taking the role of a daughter to sister to wife to mother and author, at every stage, I wanted to do my best. Never settling and an over-anxious mind created a bundle of nerves within me. I needed to get my significance, too, which is the epitome of success for a perfectionist. It's more about getting your own satisfaction and the purpose of the work. So it becomes a win-win situation, only that most of the time my winning would mean making myself and go out of the way to make things and situations look 'perfect'. I drained my energy but, of course, got appreciation and applause.

Perfectionism can be caused by **a fear of judgement or disapproval from others**. Early childhood experiences, such as having parents with unrealistically high expectations, may also play a role.

Perfectionists have unrealistic expectations of themselves. They focus on results – often unattainable ones – and are only satisfied if those results are met perfectly. They take no pride in the effort they make to achieve those results and are highly self-critical if the results are not met.

Perfectionists are in a constant loop of setting unrealistic goals and procrastinating, which leads to more denial of themselves.

All the Madam flawless reading this, please Let go of the relentless pursuit of flawlessness and instead cherish the beauty of authenticity and self-acceptance. Become more aware of yourself and strive for excellence, not perfection. In the process, enjoy the journey with a growth mindset as opposed to a fixed mindset. Most importantly, know that nobody is perfect. Learn to delegate without holding yourself to high standards.

Help Yourself

"I'm perfect in my imperfection, happy in my pain, strong in my weakness and beautiful in my own way."

I have observed that 'it's the self-talk that we do that makes an impact on our subconscious mind.

We need to learn to say enabling and empowering thoughts that make our tasks and challenges easy to achieve without overwhelming us. Our mind deciphers what we feed into it - the more positive self-affirmations we programme it with, the better outcomes and self-image we make of ourselves.

Don't wait for the perfect moment to do things perfectly!

Start doing it, make mistakes, learn through the process, be adventurous and you'll make it worth it because you have enjoyed the process and not just thought about the result and the importance it gives you.

Listing some power codes to supercharge yourself

→ My every effort is progress

→ Doing it better than perfection

→ I show up for my task, that's everything

→ I am courageous and willing to let go of my fears

→ I own my story and trust the process

→ I let go of my need for other people's approval

# 5. MS COMFY FINE

In cosy nooks where dreams reside,
Lives Ms. Comfy Fine, fears beside,
Her world is soft, with edges round,
A comfort zone where she's unbound.

She wraps herself in daily ease,
Avoids the winds of change's breeze,
Each day a mirror of the last,
Safe in the present, tied to the past.

New paths and turns she dares not tread,
Unknown futures fill her with dread,
In 'routine's arms, she finds her peace,
Yet wonders why her dreams don't cease.

She longs for more beyond the veil,
But fears the risk that change entails,
Ms. Comfy Fine, in comfort's thrall,
Yearns for courage to heed life's call.

For in the unknown lies the key,
To a life that's rich and truly free,
If she could step beyond the line,
Ms. Comfy Fine would truly shine.

This was my best description of Ms. Comfy Fine, while I stayed in my same old self, not taking challenges that made me happy. I was so safe and secure in my protective environment that I forgot who I was. Nothing kicked me out of this zone as much as this -

"she never felt ready, but she was brave and the universe responds to the brave."

Don't we all have the tendency - that small voice inside our head saying - don't do that, you'll fail, and we subconsciously accept what it tells us? We don't realise it's just telling us what we have experienced in the past. Our experiences drive us to take action today as we conclude again that we are a sum total of our thoughts and experiences.

Without taking risks, how will you learn anything new? If you never try, you'll never know. When you can connect to your true self, you open doors to change, growth, progress, love and understanding that cannot be found inside your comfort zone.

By stepping outside of your comfort zone, your horizons extend beyond what you've always known. This leads to new perspectives and perhaps a newfound sense of motivation to do something new each time you have the chance.

It's easy to do what you're used to doing and stay within the confines of least resistance, but if you want to make progress in your life, you need to break free from what holds you back, your fears, inhibitions or just your resistance to change.

We find out a lot about ourselves when we take risks. We discover what makes us tick and begin to see that part of ourselves deep inside, our true self, the one that holds the wisdom and power most of us are unaware of. The biggest challenge for us is to move out of our comfort zones because we will not grow here. Studies have shown that people who challenge themselves are excited and are sending out a signal to the universe to give them what they're aiming for in their lives.

Pushing yourself out of your comfort zone has more advantages than giving you a great story to tell your friends. The more experiences you have, the happier you will be, according to research.

Psychologists conducted a study where people documented major life events in an ongoing diary over three months, nine months and four and a half years after the events happened. "People who engage in a variety of experiences are more likely to retain positive emotions and minimise negative ones than people who have fewer experiences."

Every Ms. Comfy Fine, snug in her bubble-wrap world, may have mastered the art of cosy, but deep down, there's a daredevil waiting to skydive into the unknown. Gather the pieces of discomfort, unleash your inner thrill-seeker, and watch as life unfolds beyond the safety net of routine!

Help Yourself

"A ship is always safe at the shore, but that's not what it's built for." – Albert Einstein.

Leave your comfort zone by:

- ❖ A change in routine
- ❖ Vision an outcome for yourself
- ❖ Explore and learn
- ❖ Confront a fear
- ❖ Express yourself by showing your idea

 # 6. AUNTY PITY ME

In shadows deep, where sorrows seep,
Lives Aunty Pity Me, lost in grief,
Her world is painted shades of grey,
With pain and woe her constant stay.

She dwells within a sorrowed state,
Addicted to a mournful fate,
Each day she sings a sad refrain,
Wrapped tight in self-inflicted pain.

Aunty Pity Me, in sorrow's clasp,
Finds solace in her painful grasp,
Her heart, a well of endless cries,
Her spirit trapped in mournful ties.

Yet somewhere deep within her chest,
A spark of strength does faintly rest,
If only she could see the light,
Beyond her self-imposed night.

For in her soul, though shadows loom,
A garden waits, with flowers in bloom,
If Aunty Pity Me could break,
She'd find a world of joy to make.
Believe it and never let insecurity run your life.

Always remember that you are braver than you believe, stronger than you seem, smarter than you think and loved more than you know. The original quote came from Disney. Christopher Robin tells Pooh.

No matter how much most women give around, they do not feel their self-worth. They resist, deny and refuse praise and growth. Have you experienced this lately? Have you seen anyone go through this syndrome called *self pity*? Everyone goes through pain, everyone faces challenges. you'll be left alone in this world, pitying yourself, if you don't do this – Unlearn self pity.Don't get addicted to pain and sorrow because, in the process of getting sympathy, you're chained in your own mindset, which is that of sadness and guilt. *The astonishing part is that people find comfort in pain.*

Why? 'Because it gives them a sense of' purpose.

Why would someone do this to themselves? Only when they are not happy with the life they're leading! And who has stopped them from leading the life of their choice? Reflect on this and you'll be surprised by the reply you receive. How many barriers and negative codes do you make of yourself? Are these helping you move forward in the aspect of life you feel you're stuck in - it could be a career, relationships or health.

Every Aunty Pity Me could give masterclasses in finding comfort in sorrow, but hidden beneath the clouds of gloom is a superwoman waiting to discover the joy of saving herself. Medal your inner hero, ditch the pity party, and rewrite your life's script with a comic twist. *This is what I call being Self-ish! (not selfish)*

> *"Owning our story and loving yourself through that*
> *process is the bravest thing that we'll ever do."*

Help yourself

> ***"Adopt the peace of nature. Her secret is patience."***
> ***– Ralph Waldo Emerson.***

When nature speaks, life heals. Knowing what your dreams and passions are is the easier part. The learning part is about how to get there through roadblocks. As nature seeps within in the form of a sunrise or sunset, a beautiful flower bloom, innocent drops of rain, or just your pet buddy, dopamine releases manifold, letting you overcome the problems or stress you're going through, as there's a divine exchange of power and energy that's happening.

* Take 15 mins of your 24 hours.
* Observe a plant and talk to it.
* Lie down to observe the night sky.
* Get drenched in rain.
* Walk on grass barefoot.

Redefining Limitations

Here's a story which makes us realise how quickly we accept and sink into comfort.

Once, there lived two very different yet similarly confined creatures. One was a vibrant parrot housed in a lavish cage. Every day, his owners provided him with an assortment of foods and exquisite fruits, and he entertained them and their children with his colourful plumage and cheerful and vibrant talks. Yet, every morning, as he watched other birds soar freely through the window, he felt a deep, unshakeable disappointment. His beautiful feathers and unique voice were admired by all, but his heart yearned for the freedom he glimpsed beyond his gilded bars.

In another distant land, in a circus yard, a baby elephant was chained to a wooden post. When he first arrived, he would strain against the chain, trying to break free and explore the lush pastures he could see in the distance. But each attempt was futile; the chain was too strong, and the post too unyielding. Over time, the young elephant came to believe that the boundaries of his chain were the limits of his world. He stopped trying to break free, accepting that the only food he would eat was what came to him, and the only company he would keep was himself. As he grew into a mighty elephant, his strength increased exponentially, yet he never again tested the limits of his chain, remaining bound to his small, familiar territory.

Both the parrot and the elephant lived under the shadow of self-imposed limitations. The parrot, though physically capable of flying to the highest treetops, was mentally caged by his acceptance of his gilded prison. The elephant, despite his tremendous strength that could uproot the very post he was chained to, believed he was forever bound by the small chain that had once confined him.

These two stories intertwine to illustrate a powerful truth: our beliefs can be our greatest barriers. Just like the parrot and the elephant, we often accept the constraints placed upon us, never realising our true potential. We see the boundaries set by others or by our past failures, and we internalise them, making them our own.

Imagine if the parrot realised that the cage door was not locked or if the elephant understood his strength. Their worlds would expand in ways they had never dreamed possible. The sky would no longer be a distant hope for the parrot, and the elephant would roam freely, discovering new landscapes and companions.

The same is true for us. When we try to change our self-imposed limits and question the beliefs that hold us back, we open the door to new possibilities. Our potential is often far greater than we realise, and by breaking free from the mental chains that bind us, we can soar to heights we never thought possible.

So, let the stories of the caged parrot and the chained elephant remind us to look beyond our perceived limitations. By believing in our true capabilities, we can break free from the confines of our own making and embrace the boundless opportunities ahead of us.

**We have as many as 50,000 thoughts a day.
80% are negative, 95% repeat daily.
YOU can change that ratio.**

Most of the problems (the place where you get stuck in life) you face are created in your mind. It is also true that it's the same mind that has the capability to find solutions only if we are ready to define the issue. If you see, there is a bucket full of assorted problems in our lives. Some that are big for you may not be the same for others. Women in particular, and most of them, I would say, are fine-tuned to absorb anything that comes their way - be it conflict with their spouse, the pitfall of finances, corporate politics, envious friends, big-mouthed relatives or over-manipulative helpers.

There's this powerful antidote to solving the problem of 'stacking problems' and making a 'pity party' about it: speak to 10 people in a week, known or unknown and make a checklist of the problems they are facing.

A very effective therapy was conducted once where all the people who attended this 'pity party' had to list their problems on a sheet of paper, fold it and pass it around to exchange it with others. Here are the results:

1. Every person wanted to have their own list back. Why? Because every other person seemed to have bigger problems. They were asked to practice gratitude for all that they HAVE, instead of sulking over problems.

2. The beliefs they had, whether pertaining to health, wealth, or relationships or the negative coding which they carried like a rock on their back, got resolved when they started focusing on themselves and not the problem.

3. Every problem gets resolved when you decide to change within. There are unresolved aspects of life that we tend to carry and move sound with. Rewind and assess. Speak out to someone. Journal it. I can bet you, it will help you get clarity about yourself and what next you need to do.

Section 2

Direction

7. MIND MAGIC

The creation of man and endowing him with a brain to set him apart from other beings is the most influential force. Although we are all born equal, our dreams are different and more often than not by teenage, we stop dreaming. What happens is that people put a limitation on what we believe we can do. We possess the most powerful and efficient machines in the world, but we fail to utilise them to the best of our ability, instead filling them with negative beliefs and irrational ideologies.

Now, think of a situation in your life when you achieved something incredible and recall what you said to yourself. How did you feel about it? This is what we should be feeling every day. Every day in life is a 'present,' and it is precious. Don't just let it pass off and go. Make the most of your every living day, make yourself proud every single day.

There's a quote said by the very powerful First Lady: "There's no limit to what we as women can achieve." My mind has understood, absorbed, imbibed and accepted this—so much so that I feel I have the potential to transform many women's lives from here on. This book is like my baby that will grow and help others grow to their full potential. I would really appreciate it if you could connect with your body, mind and soul. Make your life's journey worthwhile. There's no such thing as the right thing—if you dream it, you can do it. That's the punchline to feed your brain. If you develop the ability to change from within, the entire life around you will dramatically change! Don't give in to self-talk or toxic energies that pull you back. You are capable, and you will do it to make a change in your life and make it worthwhile. Whenever such energies overpower you, replace them with positive energies of possibilities—imagine beyond your limits!

Talk to yourself constantly. That's the time the mind, which has an inbuilt mechanism of ruling your body, will give you ideas to accept or reject. All great people use their minds with the presence of heart energy and achieve spectacular results.

Defining Moments

A defining moment is a pivotal instance that shapes one's identity or direction in life.

It is often marked by inner realisation or decision-making. For women, it might be embracing motherhood, starting a successful business, or overcoming a significant personal challenge, each moment influencing their path forward with clarity and purpose. These moments crystallise values, strengths, and aspirations.

Defining moments does shape your life, marking the points where you choose to fight, persevere and transform. These pivotal experiences carve out your path, teaching you invaluable lessons and building relentless courage. Whether it's overcoming a personal loss, standing up against adversity or taking a bold leap of faith, each defining moment adds to your strength and character guiding future choices and growth.

Now let's talk about one of the defining moments we are talking about in this book – build yourself and your purpose.

Is it simple?

No

Is it overnight?

No

Will it be challenging?

Yes

Now, let's partake some hurdles that come in the way & understand them. overcoming unexpected hurdle by leveraging your strengths, seeking feedback, and maintaining a proactive approach. This is how determination and strategic thinking can lead to overcoming obstacles and achieving success.

Here are some of the common hurdles, or what I call the *Clouds of the mind.*

1. FEAR

Are there really ways when a person has taken a break and wishes to pick up the pieces of the past and move ahead? What happens when you want to do something different and bring about a change... You **Fear**.

Fear of failure

Fear of rejection

Fear of being judged

Fear of losing your comfort zone

Fear of being unable to give time like before

Fear that you will lose out on your relationships

My client Tina was once talking to me and said that she was not satisfied with the work culture and ethics and she constantly felt threatened that she was not up to it to continue in the same place. But she feared that if it was brought out from her and she would be compelled to leave the job or be removed, she feared the more drastic adjustments she would have to make in a new scenario. She thought, "It's better I stick to a place I know, as I have already invested so much time here, and the uncertainty would make me more anxious." She got stressed out and one fine day had to visit a doctor for consultation. She did her blood work, which showed abnormal lipids and sugar levels. "What have I done? I want my health back," she said in a shocked voice. There are many people like this who keep revelling in the damage that's done by ruminating thoughts and low energy. As she got guidance from me, she got a grip on handling herself, her anxieties and her health condition. She followed the guide step by step and learned to ease herself and accept problems. Instead of a tubular vision, she learned to view situations in a wider holistic approach. She discovered her tilt towards creativity and founded her brand of home made gourmet chocolates. A skill and passion unveiled.

2. SELF DOUBT

This has broken more dreams than failure ever will. Thinking that you may not make it ahead stalls you in the first step itself.

The phenomenon called self-doubt has the ability to eat into our creativity and our ability to figure out things. Feeling like you're not good enough and lacking skills had Poorna doubting herself more than a contestant on a cooking show who just burnt the water. She had been home since her maternity leave, eagerly awaiting her bundle of joy, Riya. But after the joyous arrival, Poonam found herself hit by a wave of postpartum blues that no one warned her could feel like a tsunami.

Despite delivering a healthy baby, every time she looked at Riya, she felt a surge of depression that made her question everything. She had been looking forward to the joys of motherhood, imagining diaper-changing would be a piece of cake and late-night feedings a bonding experience. Instead, she found herself overwhelmed to the point of sadness, like she'd been handed a crying, tiny boss with no off switch.

Poorna went into a shell, retreating like a turtle who suddenly decided that life on land was overrated. It took an army of friends, family and professionals to pull her out, but the seed of self-doubt had already taken root and blossomed into a full-grown, mind-invading weed.

Fast forward to today: Riya is five years old, and poorna is ready to jump back into the workforce. Armed with a fresh resume and the determination of a caffeinated squirrel, she reached out to her old job. The response? A polite but firm "no" due to the time gap in her employment.

End of all hopes? Not a chance!

Poorna decided that if life hands you a tangled mess of yarn, you don't just unravel it—you knit yourself a fabulous new sweater. She started exploring new skills, taking online courses and networking like a pro. Poorna reinvented herself, proving that a break doesn't mean broken and that a comeback can be stronger than the setback.

With us, her journey from self-doubt to self-assured was filled with laughter, a few tears and the realisation that sometimes, the only one doubting you is you. And once poorna kicked that weed of doubt to the curb, there was no stopping her.

The comfort zone sounds good, but it is a dangerous place to be in. Here, growth is hindered by comforting thoughts about yourself, and in your mind, you have accepted that your situation will surely not change. The more you resist this change, the more sad your mind and life will be. Had Poorna or Aanya decided to stay here all their lives with validating tags for themselves like, "I'm a doting mom and want to spend time with my child," or "I'm happy with spending my husband's money," or "I have accepted that I will never be able to work," would they have found their calling?

It is actually your subconscious mind (which is a *hot seat* of life's experiences and thoughts and programmed to keep you safe always) that feels threatened and makes your inner voice when you say such statements to yourself.

I experienced the dangers of staying in this zone for almost an eternity.

The ironic part is that we are happy to be in this state of comfort until time becomes uncomfortable, and it dawns on us that we have stagnated from the inside, have no will to grow and flourish, and have muffled our desires. The most important part is the awakening of the conscious mind. The direction that you give your mind to act in the way you want.

3. NO GUIDANCE

When Sonia understood that she was longing to make a difference in people's lives, as this gave her immense satisfaction, she didn't know where to begin. She was in a good position while teaching yoga and meditation at a wellness centre, and she also had a contract to conduct biweekly sessions at a prestigious corporate company. But with onset of COVID and a manifold increase in yoga instructors and her shifting away to another country made transitions difficult and created a void in her life. Have you faced this scenario when you want to move ahead for an overhaul but get stuck on your route as you feel there's no one to guide you and help you understand yourself and your goal, isn't it? Well, I have! Not uncommon, though. I sat clueless night after night, thinking about the same thing, and honestly, it used to intimidate me. This roadblock comes frequently across in the quest to find yourself, your goals, and your mission and vision.

My humble gratitude to my mentor through whose program I started getting clarity, and I'm now able to give the same back to the women who are stuck in their lives. Mentors can provide specific insights and information that enable the mentee's success. For example, they offer instructions on how to perform particular tasks or develop useful skills. Individuals starting their career can benefit from such guidance, as it helps them feel comfortable in the role more quickly

4. LACK OF COURAGE

Courage is different from confidence. An example is the weakest woman with no confidence, who will definitely find the courage to fight an animal if her child is in question. That means taking the leap of faith and finding a path no matter what.

I had found a soul sister in Sameera. Why, you ask? We were identical in our personalities and our apprehensions about moving ahead in life. She, being a nutritionist, too, connected with me instantly. She had many more years of experience than me but had to leave her job because of her own health challenges.

She had developed hypertension, which led to an abortion. Now she says, "I have lost the courage to restart any work", although she has a brilliant startup idea. With enough mentoring and compassion, I helped her get connected to a startup hub, where she is progressing now. When we act courageously, we carefully weigh the risks and rewards before moving forward, even if we're afraid. This approach not only helps us handle challenges but also opens up new ways of seeing and understanding the world around us.

5. THE CHATTERBOX MIND

Making the decision to start in search of your purpose is tough, as that's where the little voice in the mind says,
BE WHERE YOU ARE!.

This chatterbox is constantly buzzing with thoughts and opinions. It's like having a non-stop conversation going on inside your head, where every decision and every action is met with a barrage of doubts, fears, and reasons to stay put. This chatterbox is persuasive; it tells you to stick to what's comfortable, to avoid risks, and to shy away from the unknown. It's that voice saying, "Why rock the boat? You're fine where you are."

This internal dialogue can be overwhelming. It's like having a friend who means well but keeps reminding you of all the potential pitfalls and dangers of stepping into the unfamiliar. Yet, amidst all this noise, there's also a quieter voice—the one that whispers about growth, opportunity, and the fulfilment that comes from chasing your dreams.

So, navigating the chatterbox mind means learning to distinguish between its cautionary tales and the quiet nudges towards growth.

When opportunity doesn't come knocking, don't wait. Just open the door and begin your journey to find yourself.

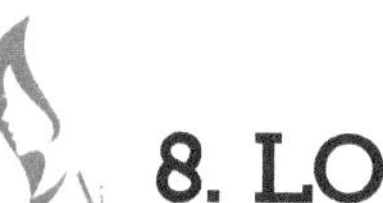# 8. LOOKING WITHIN

Why do we not get the most out of our lives? How many of you would agree that we tend to lose our individuality, our sense of purpose, our simplicity, our innocence and our nature of peace, love and kindness? Simply put, we lose our self-belief. We become different people and lead different lives. We cannot be at ease with ourselves or others if we don't re-invest ourselves with self-belief. We have a physical and spiritual power with us called *life energy*, which is lit below our dull existing surface. There is our body and our soul, just the same way as night and day or land and water. Without one, the other can't exist. As human beings, we are blessed with consciousness. By understanding and managing our minds alone, creativity will overflow with joy, love and harmony. Your body and soul together form the fabric of life. The soul is our connection with higher power, and the body stands for materialistic aspects of life.

When you shut all your sensory tools—eye, ears, nose and touch—what are you left with? YOURSELF!

Life is a continuous quest for understanding the greater meaning of our existence. When you experience unexplained anxiety, aimlessness or a void within yourself, it means your soul is craving nourishment, which comes from virtues and spreading knowledge. Just as the body seeks physical needs, our soul also lifts us towards new and loftier heights.

Section 3

Design

DESIGN

"You are allowed to reintroduce yourself to the universe as you heal. The pieces you put back together have much to reveal."

As we journey through life, may we always remember that true happiness is not found in the pursuit of external pleasures but in the quiet moments of connection, gratitude and love.

Happiness is that radiant force emanating from the depths of your soul, infusing every moment with warmth and light. It's the gentle whisper of contentment that echoes through your being, reminding you that life is a gift to be cherished.

Consider the simple joys of a child's laughter or the beauty of a sunrise painting the sky with hues of gold and pink. These are the moments that remind us of the magic that exists in the world if only we take the time to notice.

In the words of Mahatma Gandhi, "Happiness is when what you think, what you say and what you do are in harmony." It's about finding alignment between your thoughts, words, and actions and living in accordance with your truest self.

Research shows that happiness isn't just a fleeting emotion; it's a powerful state of being that has manifold effects on our health and well-being. Studies have found that happy people tend to live longer, have stronger immune systems and experience lower levels of stress and anxiety.

But perhaps the most beautiful thing about happiness is its ability to ripple outwards, touching the lives of everyone it encounters. Think of the friend who always has a smile on their face or the stranger who offers a kind word of encouragement when you need it most. These are the moments that remind us of the transformative power of happiness.

As Desmond Tutu once said, "Do your little bit of good where you are; it's those little bits of good put together that overwhelm the world." When we cultivate happiness within ourselves, we become torch bearers, spreading love and positivity to all those around us.

9. FINDING THE CAUSE OF THE CAUSE

Are you satisfied today?

Did you ever realise that the daily work you do, whether at home or in the office, can make everything so mundane and monotonous that the spark of fun or enjoyment gets missed out?

Day in and day out, the same routine is not an exciting moment for the millions of neurons that wake up with you. When your brain senses familiarity in the train of thoughts that you have from the minute you rise out of bed, half the neurons go off to sleep again because they don't have anything new or exciting to do or anything that will make you excited, energetic and satisfied. When this pattern gets repeated over the years, their excitability is zero and work tends to stagnate, suffocate, and suffer and the result is your dissatisfaction. Most of us become okay with doing this.

a. Lost Connection

As a wellness coach, I often see women struggling with a lot of despair rooted in the disconnection between their minds and bodies. This detachment leaves you feeling fragmented, like a ship adrift without an anchor. When your mind is constantly racing, filled with worries and stress, while your body feels tense and neglected, it creates a vicious cycle of discomfort and unease. This disconnection can manifest in various ways—chronic fatigue, anxiety and a general sense of being out of sync with yourself. It's as if your mind and body are speaking different languages and are unable to communicate effectively. Recognising this disconnection is crucial. It's a signal that you need to start listening to your body, practising mindfulness and finding ways to reconnect these integral parts of yourself. Simple practices like deep breathing, yoga, or mindful walking can help bridge this gap, bringing you back to a state of harmony and reducing the despair you feel.

b. Silent Saboteur

A guilty conscience can be a relentless source of despair. It's like carrying a heavy backpack filled with regrets, self-criticism and unspoken apologies. This burden drags you down, making it difficult to find joy or peace in your daily life. Guilt often stems from past mistakes, perceived failures and harsh self-judgements. It creates a toxic cycle of self-blame and negative thinking, where you constantly replay past actions and criticise yourself for them. This relentless self-criticism can be paralysing, preventing you from moving forward. As a coach, I encourage you to acknowledge these feelings without judgement. Understand that holding onto guilt serves no purpose other than to keep you stuck.

Begin practising self-compassion and forgiveness. Write down your feelings of guilt, and then consciously release them, perhaps through a symbolic act like tearing up the paper. By letting go of guilt, you open the door to healing and allow yourself to embrace a future free from the chains of the past.

c. The Shadows of Judgement

Living under the shadow of constant judgement can lead to profound despair. This judgement can be directed both inwardly and outwardly, creating a toxic environment where no one, including yourself, is ever good enough. When you judge others harshly, it often reflects your insecurities and fears. It's a defence mechanism that isolates you, making you feel superior yet profoundly alone. This constant criticism breeds a sense of isolation and inadequacy. As a coach, I urge you to pause and reflect whenever you catch yourself judging. Consider your own journey and the mistakes you've made. Use this moment to practise empathy and self-reflection. Understand that every woman you meet is fighting her own battles, just like you. By choosing understanding and compassion over judgement, you create a more supportive and inclusive environment, which in turn lightens your own heart and reduces the despair you feel.

d. Envy: A Poison to the Soul

Envy is a silent yet potent poison that eats away at your soul, leading to deep-seated despair. When you constantly compare yourself to others and feel envious, it diminishes your self-worth and breeds resentment. Envy blinds you to your own unique qualities and achievements, making you feel perpetually inadequate.

This state of mind prevents you from appreciating your journey and celebrating your successes. When you feel envious of someone, examine what it is you admire about them. Is it their confidence, success or happiness? Use these observations as motivation to set your own goals and work towards them. Celebrate the achievements of others as a reminder that you, too, can reach your aspirations with dedication and effort. Uplift yourself and engage in activities that fuel your passion. Let envy be the spark that ignites your drive for personal success rather than a source of despair.

e. Anchored with Resistance

resistance to change is a common yet significant cause of despair. It keeps you stuck in unfulfilling patterns and prevents personal growth. Fear of the unknown and a desire for control can make you resist the very changes that could bring joy and fulfilment into your life. This resistance creates a sense of stagnation, where you feel trapped in a monotonous routine with no way out.

As a wellness coach, I emphasise the importance of embracing change.

Start small, with achievable goals that gradually expand your comfort zone. Embrace the mantra: "Change is a process, not an event." Reflect on past experiences where change led to positive outcomes. Trust in your ability to adapt and grow. Create a vision board that visualises your goals and dreams, reminding you daily of the possibilities ahead. Celebrate each small step you take towards embracing change. By overcoming resistance, you open yourself to new opportunities and a life filled with growth and fulfilment, moving away from despair and towards empowerment.

e. Holding on to Hot Coals

Imagine holding a hot coal in your hand. The longer you hold onto it, the more it burns you. Anger, anxiety, disgust and resentment are like those hot coals—they hurt you more than anyone else. These emotions can cloud your vision, create unnecessary stress and hinder your personal growth and progress in every area of your life.

These often stem from unmet expectations or fear of the unknown. While it's natural to feel these emotions, allowing them to control your actions can lead to destructive outcomes. Disgust and hate towards yourself or others can build barriers. These emotions can prevent you from seeing situations clearly and making rational decisions. Practice empathy and forgiveness, not just for others but for yourself as well. Letting go of these negative feelings can open the door to new opportunities, unleashing you from the pattern of a seemingly uneasy state of self.

your core being should be free of such 'core infesting bugs'. Realising any of the above causes can be the turning point, from where you can turn the tables in your favour.

10. TRIAD MODEL OF BEING YOU

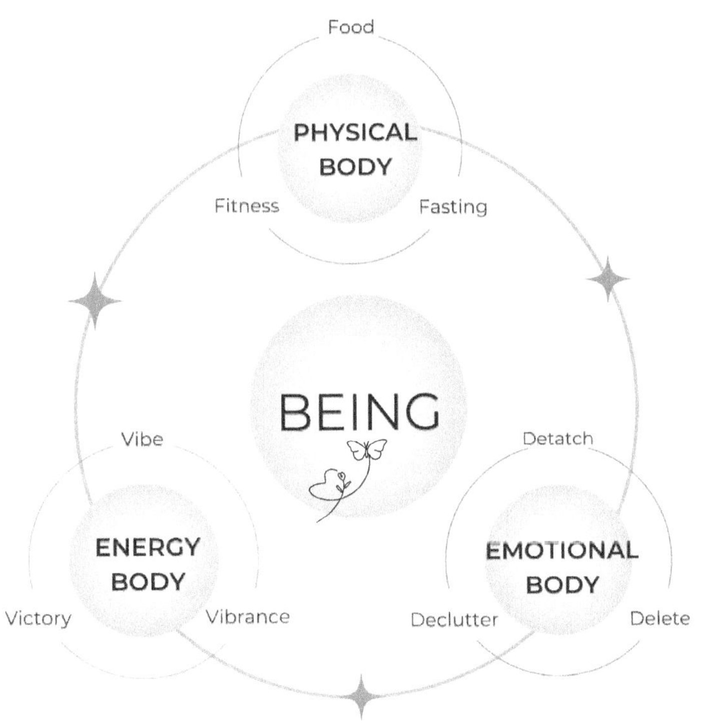

1. Physical Body

Healing the physical body is essential for transforming our visible energy and achieving our dreams. When we provide our bodies with the right nourishment—balanced nutrition, adequate hydration and regular physical activity—we cultivate vitality and strength. This physical well-being radiates as visible energy, enhancing our presence and charisma. A well-nourished body supports mental clarity, emotional stability and resilience, empowering us to pursue our goals with enthusiasm and determination.

By prioritising our physical health, we lay a solid foundation for overall well-being, enabling us to reach our highest potential and turn our dreams into reality.

3 Dimensions of Physical Body

- ❖ Fitness,
- ❖ Food and
- ❖ Fasting

Fitness to Energise:

Cardiovascular Exercises:

Cardiovascular health is crucial for overall wellness. Incorporate activities like brisk walking, jogging, cycling or swimming. For example, you might start with a 30-minute brisk walk on Mondays and progress to jogging or cycling as you build endurance. High-intensity interval training (HIIT) can be particularly effective and time-efficient.

Strength Training:

Building muscle and bone density is vital for women, especially to prevent osteoporosis. Include resistance training with weights or bodyweight exercises like squats, lunges, push-ups and planks on Wednesdays. Use resistance bands or kettlebells for added variety and challenge.

Yoga/Flexibility Routines:

Flexibility exercises improve the range of motion and reduce injury risk. Practice yoga or Pilates on Fridays to enhance flexibility, balance and relaxation. Incorporate poses like downward dog, child's pose, warrior sequences and stretches targeting major muscle groups.

Somatic Exercises:

Somatic exercises address nervous system dysregulation, which is common in women due to stress and multitasking. Integrate gentle movements like shoulder rolls, swaying and rocking back and forth to release tension and improve mind-body connection. Practices such as Feldenkrais or Alexander Technique can be particularly beneficial.

Track Your Progress:

❖ Use fitness apps, a Fitbit/smartwatch, or keep a detailed journal to log your workouts and monitor your progress.

❖ Set specific, measurable goals such as running a 5K in three months, lifting a certain weight or mastering a challenging yoga pose.

❖ Celebrate milestones like increased endurance, strength or flexibility. Reward yourself with a treat like a massage, a new workout outfit or a special outing when you hit your targets.

Foods that Nourish:

Meal Planning:

Embrace diverse dietary practices from around the world to enhance nutrition and enjoyment. For example, Mediterranean diets focus on healthy fats like olive oil, fish and plenty of vegetables, while Japanese diets emphasise seafood, rice and fermented foods. Incorporating a variety of cuisines can ensure a balanced intake of nutrients.

Nutrient-Dense Foods:

Focus on nutrient-dense foods that provide essential vitamins and minerals. Include a variety of colourful vegetables (leafy greens, bell peppers, carrots), lean proteins (chicken, fish, legumes, tofu), and whole grains (quinoa, brown rice, oats).

Superfood supplements: Incorporate superfoods known for their high nutrient content, such as chia seeds, flaxseeds, berries, nuts and dark leafy greens. These foods can enhance energy levels, improve digestion and support overall health.

Detoxifying Foods: Include foods known for their detoxifying properties, such as cruciferous vegetables (broccoli, cauliflower, kale), citrus fruits (lemons, oranges), garlic, ginger and green tea. These foods help support liver function and aid in the elimination of toxins from the body.

Cultural Variations: Respect cultural food preferences and availability. For example, in regions where fish is more accessible than meat, prioritise seafood for protein. In tropical areas, utilise local fruits like mangoes, papayas and coconuts for their nutritional benefits.

Mindful Eating Practices

Mindful Eating Techniques: Eat slowly and savour each bite, focusing on the textures and flavours of your food. Chew thoroughly and listen to your body's hunger and fullness signals to prevent overeating.

Incorporate cultural eating rituals that promote mindfulness, such as the Japanese practice of "Hara Hachi Bu," which means eating until you are 80% full, or the Mediterranean tradition of communal meals that emphasise slow eating and social connection.

Distraction-Free Eating: Avoid distractions like TV or phones during meals to fully enjoy your food. This can help improve digestion and increase satisfaction with your meals.

Fasting to Renew

Fasting as Detox: Incorporate intermittent fasting into your routine as a form of detoxification. Try a 16:8 fasting schedule, where you fast for 16 hours and eat during an 8-hour window. For example, eat between 12 PM and 8 PM. This can help improve metabolism, promote weight loss and support cellular repair and regeneration.

Hydration and Nutrient Balance: Drink plenty of water, herbal teas and electrolyte-rich drinks during fasting periods to stay hydrated and support detoxification processes. Ensure that your meals during the eating window are nutrient-dense to maintain energy levels and provide essential vitamins and minerals for detoxification.

Detox from Specific Negative Energies: Surround yourself with positive influences and minimise exposure to toxic relationships or environments. Practice setting healthy boundaries and saying no to things that drain your energy or cause stress. Incorporate energy-clearing practices like smudging with sage or palo santo, using crystals or visualisation techniques to release negative energy and promote balance and harmony.

By identifying these aspects as the root causes of despair, you can begin to address and overcome them.

Each step towards understanding and healing these issues brings you closer to a life filled with peace and fulfilment.

You have the power to transform despair into hope and resilience. Remember, every journey begins with a single step, and you are never alone on this path to wellness.

2. Emotional Body

The emotional body of being is where our feelings, memories, and emotional patterns reside. It influences how we experience and process emotions, affecting our mental health and interpersonal relationships.

3. Dimensions of emotional body
Delete:

❖ Negative Thought Patterns: Identify negative thoughts and replace them with positive affirmations. For instance, change "I can't do this" to "I am capable and strong."

❖ Emotional Release Techniques: Practice techniques such as journaling, where you write out your feelings daily or use guided meditations to help process and release emotional burdens.

❖ Emotional Freedom Techniques (EFT): Incorporate EFT tapping sessions into your routine to release emotional blockages. Spend a few minutes tapping on specific meridian points on your body while voicing affirmations or addressing stress and anxiety. This can help alleviate emotional distress and promote emotional balance.

Declutter:

❖ Toxic Relationships: Evaluate your relationships and set boundaries with people who drain your energy. Prioritise time with those who support and uplift you. If necessary, seek support from a therapist to navigate complex relationships.

❖ Emotional Clarity Exercises: Engage in activities like mindful breathing exercises or guided imagery to clear emotional clutter. Set aside 10 minutes each day for these practices to maintain emotional clarity.

❖ Content Detox: Take breaks from social media, news and other sources that contain negative or overwhelming content. Limit exposure to content that triggers negative emotions and focus on uplifting and inspiring material like reading books or listening to podcasts, practising mindfulness or meditation, spending time in nature or pursuing creative hobbies.

Detach:

❖ Mindfulness Practices: Incorporate daily mindfulness practices such as 10 minutes of meditation focused on the present moment. Use apps like Headspace or Calm to guide you if needed.

❖ Acceptance and Letting Go: Practice acceptance by recognising what you cannot control and letting go of the need to manage every outcome. Engage in activities that reinforce this mindset, like yoga or tai chi, which emphasise flow and acceptance.

❖ Creative Visualisation: Use the power of the mind's eye exercises to release negative energy and promote emotional balance.

By incorporating emotional wellness practices, you can enhance your ability to release emotional blockages and achieve greater emotional balance and resilience. This integrated approach can empower you by boosting your confidence, stamina, and ability to handle the demands of professional life effectively. It sets a foundation for a balanced, healthy lifestyle that supports both personal and career growth.

3. Energy Body

The energy body of being is composed of the subtle energy fields that flow through and around us. It plays a crucial role in maintaining our overall vitality and balance, impacting how we feel physically, emotionally, and spiritually.

3 dimensionsof energy body

❖ Vibe

❖ Vibrance

❖ Victory

As an author and coach dedicated to empowering women, I firmly believe that true transformation goes beyond the physical realm and extends into the vibrant energy that courses through our beings. Let's delve into the dimensions of elevating your energy body, igniting your inner vibrance and embracing the power of purpose.

Vibe Enhancement:

❖ Home Environment: Create a space that uplifts your spirit and nourishes your soul. Declutter your surroundings, infuse them with soothing colours, and adorn them with elements that resonate with your essence.

❖ Daily Energy Rituals: Establish a morning routine that sets the tone for positivity and success. Start your day with affirmations, visualisation or meditation to align your energy with your intentions.

Vibrance Activation:

❖ Self-Care Regimen: Prioritise self-care practices that recharge your energy and radiance. Indulge in activities that bring you joy, whether it's pampering yourself with skincare rituals, enjoying nature walks or immersing yourself in creative pursuits.

❖ Power of Purpose: Discover and align with your life's purpose. When you live in alignment with your passions and values, you unleash a boundless reservoir of energy and enthusiasm. Embrace the journey of self-discovery and pursue endeavours that ignite your soul.

Victory Manifestation:

Community of like minded people and passion - A mastermind circle will fill the gap of jigsaw puzzle when you falter or lose track. Always learn give and take empowerment.

❖ Gratitude Integration: Cultivate a mindset of gratitude to amplify positivity and attract abundance into your life. Keep a gratitude journal and regularly reflect on the blessings and victories, no matter how small, that grace your path.

❖ Energy Alchemy: Transform negative energies into sources of empowerment. It comes within a matter of a moment. The energy shift is faster than the physical shift, just like moving down a wormhole. It takes you to unsolved territories where your energies are maximum.

Through intentional practices and a commitment to harnessing the power of your energy body, you can elevate your vibrance, unlock your inner radiance and step into your full potential. Embrace the journey with conviction and confidence, knowing that you possess the innate power to shape your reality and manifest your dreams.

Real-life heroes who conquered their lives

A few years back, Mihika and Sultana found themselves at the crossroads of despair and hope, their lives intertwined by the common thread of struggle and resilience.

Mihika's life took a dramatic turn after a severe accident left her with chronic back pain. This misfortune was compounded by the loss of her job at an interior firm where she had worked for ten years, a position that had been a cornerstone of her identity. Her home, once filled with warmth, became a battleground of frustration and anger. Her only daughter, accustomed to a different kind of attention, now bore the brunt of Mihika's emotional turmoil. The yelling and blame games created an atmosphere thick with tension, leaving the once-happy home in a state of disarray.

Around the same time, Sultana was embarking on a new chapter of her life. Recently married, she moved to the Gulf, leaving behind her job in finance in India, a role that never truly fulfilled her. Though excited about her marriage, Sultana was apprehensive about her new life abroad. Her concerns were not just emotional but also physical; she had recently been diagnosed with PCOS, a condition that added to her stress and uncertainty.

Their paths converged when both women sought my help as a coach. Determined to reclaim their lives, they embarked on a journey of holistic healing together. We started with the basics: decluttering their environments to create spaces that fostered peace and positivity. Both Mihika and Sultana began journaling, using the practice to pour out their frustrations and chart their paths to recovery.

Nutrition played a crucial role in their transformation. We crafted diets rich in wholesome, nourishing foods that supported their physical health. Regular fitness routines were also introduced, tailored to Mihika's back condition and Sultana's PCOS. These physical changes were complemented by mental and emotional practices, particularly the daily habit of gratitude. By focusing on the positives, they began to see the world and their circumstances in a new light.

Mihika's turnaround was nothing short of remarkable. Not only did she reverse her chronic back pain, but she also discovered a newfound passion for Indian classical dance. She began teaching from her home, creating "Aunty Mihika's Graceful Souls," a space where little girls gathered to learn dance and share in the joy that radiated from Mihika's heart. The once tense household was now a scene of laughter and creativity.

Meanwhile, Sultana found her calling in an unexpected place. During her job search in the Gulf, she stumbled upon an online portal for teaching maths to high school students using innovative techniques. This opportunity reignited her passion for maths and gave her a sense of purpose and fulfilment that her previous job had lacked. Teaching became more than just a profession; it was a source of joy and a way to connect deeply with her students.

Through their journeys, Mihika and Sultana became each other's pillars of support. They shared their struggles and triumphs, drawing strength from their shared experiences. As they healed, they not only transformed their own lives but also inspired those around them. Their stories are a testament to the power of resilience and the profound impact of holistic healing.

Together, they learned that true happiness and fulfilment come from within. By taking care of their physical and mental well-being, Mihika and Sultana were able to radiate positivity and create ripples of joy in their communities. They found a purpose for living. Their intertwined stories serve as a powerful reminder that, even in the face of adversity, it is possible to find light and spread it to others.

11. DREAMS

A DREAM THAT YOU SEE WITH YOUR EYES OPEN

DO NOT ALLOW ANYONE TO STEAL YOUR DREAMS. KEEP YOUR DREAMS, MAGNIFY YOUR DREAMS. ACT UPON YOUR DREAMS AND MAKE THEM A REALITY.

Are you constantly feeling that life in the second innings is a struggle

And my story continues… OH, YOU'RE JUST A HOMEMAKER!

There's no denying that a stay-at-home mom is the most demanding, most rewarding, most satisfying, most validated and considered the first school a child is born into. It gives a sense of belongingness, love, joy and nurturing. I learned a lot of this from my parents and siblings, who love me unconditionally.

But I wasn't at all prepared to be called that all my life. I dreamed of being a healer, a changemaker. I made the most of every small opportunity. Ironically enough, unknowingly I became a health adviser to relatives, to my own family, my siblings, my friends and took up the challenge with my own in-laws who were old and needed the support for health and nutrition.

This changed my inner self. In my mind, I thought that even though I was not in a formal work setup, my inherent nature of easing out people's pain kept me up to date with my work and with myself.

The desire to design my life.

With passing time and additional responsibilities, the hiatus with my work getting bigger by the day, I feared that I wouldn't be able to fulfil my aspirations. That's the most crushing and debilitating feeling that pierced me. From time to time, I kept picking up the pieces in my life, only to be discouraged and weighed down by social pressure and by becoming an ideal stay-at-home mum. Imagine dedicating yourself wholeheartedly as a healthcare professional, working to restore hope and health in your patients' lives. Witnessing their tears of joy as they regain resilience and trust in their recovery. Yet, despite these efforts, feeling disregarded can be disheartening. Moments like these led me to seek a path where I could shape my life consciously, not by default. It's not about selfishness but about recognising the value of dedication and empathy in my work.

One particular day, as I was deep in my own dungeon, varying everything in and around my life, nothing around me making any sense, dull and bored, with a sense of emptiness. This went on for a few months before my spouse noticed. He was curious about my state of mind and temperaments. What was it that wasn't satisfying me? What was it that made it look like I was just doing my daily work mundanely and just on the surface without being emotionally or mentally involved? What is it that's made me sad and uninterested? His next question came as a shock—was it because I haven't been connected to the career that's haunting me? By then, it was almost 15 years since I had been away from my profession as a clinical dietician. In my mind, thoughts raced and I palpitated— What should I say? Would it be right to say yes? Didn't I just make a mark of being an ideal woman who's happy in her home? Should I or should I not? And I did ---- I said yes. That's when my journey began. I upgraded my skills and studied Holistic Nutrition with my newfound mentor. This gave me new vigour as I found a mastermind circle. It was the most accomplished education I have had so far, as I got recognised and offered accolades recognising my work. God has been kind and showered me with the right path.

The sense of incompleteness that most of you experience is valid, but if you keep staying incomplete, you will eventually lose respect for yourself and for others. Start doing things that you like, even if it's for 10 minutes a day—make art, listen to the music you like, write something, observe nature. Whatever it is, start to make time for yourself. When you go within, that's when the change occurs.

Through this book, you will find that little commonality that binds all of us women together, that something with which you will resonate and understand yourself too. Somewhere you will feel it's never too late; hope is always there till you live, and hopelessness kills every dream. There are so many women I have been coming across who want to do something but just end up justifying themselves.

They have lost the joy of finding themselves. This is what hurts and pains the most. Don't lose the spark that makes you who you are—make yourself proud, make the mother in you shine, or the wife in you beam with pride, and the sister in you ignite with energy.

You will not lose these identities; only you will make them strong and respectful.

It all begins with looking at the available options closely, with an open mind. In this golden era of technology and online presence, it is easier for people to pursue a passion. When earlier doing a class or consultation or tutorial was a once-in-a-blue-moon occurrence, today it is booming all over the place. At this point in time, it is essential to introspect and understand what and where you are. You have the ability to win and to live life to the fullest. We tend to fear others and live for them. With every little step you take, in hindsight, you have a feeling about what people would say.

Some of us don't live our dreams because we are busy living our fears.

I would say it's a very obvious fact that every human being in this world, no matter how rich or poor, has a spark. Yet we leave this world without realising it. For most people, dreaming is just wishful thinking, that is, they sit and wish but fail to take action, waiting for a miracle to happen. The answer is that success only comes to those who believe in it and take measurable actions and smaller steps in achieving their dreams.

The future belongs to those who believe in the beauty of their dreams.

Since I was unable to figure out a way to start doing things I wanted because of a lot of cobwebs I was carrying in my mind, I lost precious time, made blunders, lost hope many times but didn't lose sight of my outcome. I had this inner urge to help people and make a difference in their lives by transforming their health since that came to me like second nature being a nutritionist, and now being a coach was even more of a reward.

So I decided to de-weed and declutter myself first and hit the road with a life-transforming programme. Indeed, it became a game changer for me. Life got supercharged, and I started feeling better when I shed my negative self-image and broke a few barriers and beliefs that were not serving me at all. I began to bloom from a bud to a flower. Here's when I also engaged in productive learning through practical and online courses, built more credibility through social media and ventured into coaching clients across the globe. My aura and energy became better when I made friends, collaborated and moved around in a mastermind circle.

Dreams: The Fuel That Keeps You Awake

Dreams are often described as aspirations or desires so powerful that they refuse to let you rest. They stir something deep within, creating a relentless drive that pushes you to pursue them with passion and determination. For women embarking on their second innings in their careers, this metaphor of a dream can be particularly inspiring and relevant.

The Unseen Power of Dreams

1. Unyielding Motivation: A dream that doesn't allow you to sleep symbolises a level of motivation that is unyielding. It's the kind of drive that keeps you up at night, planning,

strategising and envisioning your future. For women restarting their careers, harnessing this internal fire can provide the momentum needed to overcome obstacles and persist through challenges.

2. Resilience in the Face of Adversity: When your dream is powerful enough, setbacks become temporary roadblocks rather than insurmountable barriers. This perspective is crucial for women who may face doubts, societal pressures or internal fears. A dream that won't let you sleep is a reminder that resilience and perseverance are key to turning aspirations into reality.

3. Rediscovering Passion: After a career break, it can be difficult to reconnect with one's professional identity. However, a strong, unrelenting dream can reignite old passions and uncover new ones. This process of rediscovery can be transformative, allowing women to align their career paths with what truly excites and fulfils them.

4. Breaking Comfort Zones: Dreams often push you out of your comfort zone, urging you to take risks and embrace change. For women stepping back into their careers, this means seeking new opportunities, learning new skills and challenging the status quo. Embracing this discomfort can lead to significant personal and professional growth.

Practical Steps to Realise Your Dreams

1. Clarity of Vision: Start by defining your dream in clear, concrete terms. What do you want to achieve? What does success look like to you? This clarity will help direct your efforts and keep you focused.

2. Setting Mini Goals: Break down your dream into smaller, manageable goals. Each milestone achieved brings you closer to your ultimate aspiration, providing motivation and a sense of accomplishment along the way.

3. Seek Support: Surround yourself with a supportive network of friends, family, mentors and peers. Their encouragement

and advice can be invaluable as you navigate the challenges of restarting your career.

4. Invest in Yourself: Continuously invest in your personal and professional development. Whether it's through formal education, online courses or self-study, expanding your knowledge and skills will empower you to pursue your dream with confidence.

5. Persist to Perform: Remember that setbacks are part of the journey. Stay persistent and keep your dream in sight. Use each challenge as a learning opportunity and a stepping stone towards your goal.

"If I can heal a life and stop that heart from breaking, I shall live in bliss."

a. Additional Reads

i) **Defining Moments:** Shaping the Course of Life Defining moments are pivotal experiences that shape and define individuals' lives, both positively and negatively. These moments can range from significant achievements and milestones to profound challenges and setbacks. Here's a brief note on defining moments and their impact on people's lives:

Positive Defining Moments (Blessings)

1. Achievements and Milestones: Graduating from college, landing a dream job or winning an award can be defining moments that validate hard work and dedication, boosting confidence and self-esteem.

2. Personal Growth and Discovery: Overcoming challenges, embarking on new adventures or discovering hidden talents can lead to moments of profound self-awareness and growth, shaping individuals' identities and aspirations.

3. Relationship Milestones: Falling in love, getting married or starting a family can mark transformative moments that deepen connections and bring immense joy and fulfilment.

Negative Defining Moments (Challenges)

1. Loss and Grief: Experiencing the loss of a loved one, a job, or a significant relationship can be profoundly challenging, causing grief, sadness and a reassessment of one's priorities and values.

2. Failure and Setbacks: Facing rejection, failure or setbacks in personal or professional endeavours can be humbling and discouraging, but these moments also offer valuable lessons and opportunities for resilience and growth.

3. Trauma and Crisis: Surviving traumatic events such as accidents, natural disasters, or serious illnesses can leave lasting scars, but they can also cultivate strength, resilience and a deeper appreciation for life's fragility.

Impact on People's Lives:

Identity Formation: Defining moments play a crucial role in shaping individuals' identities, values, and beliefs, influencing their sense of self and purpose in life.

Decision-Making: These moments often serve as reference points for decision-making, guiding individuals' choices and actions as they navigate future challenges and opportunities.

Personal Growth and Resilience: While good defining moments can inspire confidence and motivation, bad defining moments can foster resilience, empathy and a deeper understanding of one's capacity to overcome adversity.

Relationship Dynamics: Shared defining moments can strengthen bonds between individuals, fostering deeper connections and shared memories that endure through time.

Whether positive or negative, defining moments have an immense impact on people's lives, shaping their identities, values and relationships. By accepting these moments with resilience, introspection, and openness to growth, individuals can harness their powers to navigate life's journey with purpose and resilience.

Defining moments serve as poignant reminders of the highs and lows of the human experience, offering opportunities for reflection, growth and renewal.

ii) Who Are You - The Enneagram consists of a 9-point diagram made up of three elements: the outer circle, inner triangle and innermost hexagon. Beyond the 9 personality types, it grows more complex and includes 27 different subtypes, and the respective centres are focused on ACTION, FEELING, & THINKING.

It works well by sorting people and gives an insight into the individual's own personality, but it also provides valuable information on how to better relate to other people and improve interpersonal skills at home or at the workplace. This can be successfully applied for personal growth and development, interpersonal communications and leadership management.

The Enneagram is a powerful scientific tool for understanding personality types, offering deep insights into the core motivations, fears and desires that drive human behaviour. It divides personalities into nine distinct types, each with its own unique set of characteristics and worldviews. Here's a description of each Enneagram type:

Type - 1: The Reformer - Core Motivation: To be good, ethical and right. Core Fear: Being corrupt, evil or defective. Key Traits: Principled, purposeful, self-controlled and perfectionistic. Reformers strive for improvement and uphold high standards. They can be critical of themselves and others, aiming to avoid mistakes and ensure things are done correctly.

Type - 2: The Helper - Core Motivation: To feel loved and appreciated. Core Fear: Being unwanted or unworthy of love. Key Traits: Caring, generous and people-pleasing. Helpers are empathetic and supportive, often putting others' needs before their own. They seek approval and can struggle with setting boundaries.

Type - 3: The Achiever - Core Motivation: To feel valuable and worthwhile. Core Fear: Being worthless or a failure. Key Traits: Ambitious, adaptable and image-conscious. Achievers are goal-oriented and driven by success. They are skilled at presenting themselves in a positive light but may struggle with authenticity.

Type - 4: The Individualist - Core Motivation: To find themselves and their unique significance. Core Fear: Having no identity or personal significance. Key Traits: Introspective, expressive and sensitive. Individualists seek to understand their emotions and are often creative. They can feel misunderstood and long for deep connections and meaning.

Type - 5: The Investigator - Core Motivation: To be competent and self-sufficient. Core Fear: Being helpless or incapable. Key Traits: Analytical, perceptive and private. Investigators value knowledge and seek to understand the world. They can be detached and reserved, preferring to observe rather than participate.

Type - 6: The Loyalist - Core Motivation: To feel secure and supported. Core Fear: Being without support or guidance. Key Traits: Loyal, responsible and anxious. Loyalists are cautious and prepared for potential challenges. They seek stability and can be sceptical, often relying on trusted authorities and friends.

Type - 7: The Visionary - Core Motivation: To experience life to the fullest and avoid pain. Core Fear: Being deprived or in pain. Key Traits: Spontaneous, adventurous and optimistic. Visionaries are playful and seek new experiences. They can be easily distracted and may struggle with commitment and follow-through.

Type - 8: The Challenger - Core Motivation: To be self-reliant and strong. Core Fear: Being controlled or harmed by others. Key Traits: Assertive, protective and decisive. Challengers value control and independence. They are confident leaders but can be confrontational and struggle with vulnerability.

Type - 9: The Peacemaker - Core Motivation: To maintain peace and harmony. Core Fear: Conflict and disconnection. Key Traits: Easy-going, accommodating and receptive.

Peacemakers seek to avoid conflict and promote harmony. They are accepting and can sometimes neglect their own needs to keep the peace.

By identifying with one of these nine types, people can gain insights into their strengths and areas for growth, fostering personal development and improving relationships.

iii) Decode the code: Distress Coding vs. Power Coding: Cultivating a Mindset of Growth

Distress Coding - (D Coding) Distress coding refers to ingrained patterns of thinking and belief systems that hold us back from reaching our full potential. These negative thought patterns often stem from past experiences, societal conditioning and self-limiting beliefs. Examples include thoughts of self-sabotage, incompetence and a focus on limitations rather than possibilities.

Power Coding - (P Coding) Power coding, on the other hand, involves cultivating a mindset of growth, resilience and self-empowerment. It entails consciously rewiring our brains to focus on positive thoughts, beliefs and actions that align with our goals and aspirations. This process involves pruning old, negative patterns of thinking and nurturing new, empowering ones that support our personal growth and well-being.

12. CLEARING THE CANVAS AND PAINTING NEW HORIZONS

1. Identifying Negative Patterns: The first step in power coding is to identify and acknowledge the negative patterns of thinking and behaviour that no longer serve us. This requires self-awareness and introspection to recognise recurring thought patterns and beliefs that hold us back.

2. Challenging Limiting Beliefs: Once identified, we can challenge these limiting beliefs by examining their validity and reframing them in a more empowering light. This involves questioning the evidence supporting these beliefs and replacing them with more positive, affirming thoughts.

3. Cultivating Empowering Habits: Empowering coding involves consciously cultivating habits and practices that support our growth and well-being. This may include daily affirmations, visualisation exercises, mindfulness practices and seeking out positive influences and environments.

4. Consistent Practice and Reinforcement: Like any skill, power-coded affirmations require consistent practice and reinforcement. By consciously choosing empowering thoughts and behaviours, we strengthen neural pathways associated with positive thinking and resilience, gradually rewiring our brains for greater empowerment and success.

Negative coding can keep us stuck in patterns of pessimism and limitation, while empowered coding unlocks our full potential and paves the way for personal growth and fulfilment. By pruning old, negative patterns of thinking and nurturing new, empowering ones, we can cultivate a mindset of resilience, optimism and self-empowerment that propels us toward our goals and aspirations.

Power coding of the mind is a transformative journey that empowers individuals to break free from self-imposed limitations and embrace their full potential. Through conscious effort and practice, we can rewire our brains for greater resilience, optimism and empowerment, paving the way for a life filled with purpose, fulfilment and success.

a. Exploring Your Second Innings Success Channels

Expertise and Credentials

1. **Get Back into Your Former Role:**
   - ❖ Spruce up your resume and LinkedIn profile.
   - ❖ Reconnect with old colleagues and employers.
   - ❖ Attend industry events and seminars to get back in the groove.

2. **Boost Your Professional Skills:**
   - ❖ Take refresher courses or get relevant certifications.
   - ❖ Join professional associations and online communities.
   - ❖ Stay up to date by subscribing to industry journals and newsletters.

3. **Try Freelancing/Consulting:**
   - ❖ Offer consulting or freelancing services based on your expertise.
   - ❖ Create a portfolio showcasing your past accomplishments.
   - ❖ Build a professional website to attract clients.

Passion Meets Proficiency

1. **Start Your Own Venture:**
   - ❖ Use your qualifications to kick-start a business aligned with your passion.

- ❖ Develop a solid business plan and seek mentorship or funding.
- ❖ Utilise online platforms to market and sell your products or services.

2. Become an Educator/Trainer:

- ❖ Share your expertise by becoming a trainer or instructor.
- ❖ Conduct workshops, webinars or online courses.
- ❖ Collaborate with educational institutions or corporate training programmes.

3. Pursue Creative Endeavours:

- ❖ Combine your skills with a love for writing, art or design.
- ❖ Start a blog, publish articles or create a YouTube channel.
- ❖ Offer specialised services like graphic design, content creation or interior design.

New Horizons

1. Seek Further Education:

- ❖ Enrol in new courses or degree programmes in a different field of interest.
- ❖ Take online classes or attend workshops to acquire new skills.
- ❖ Gain hands-on experience through internships or volunteer opportunities.

2. Engage in Career Transition Programmes:

- ❖ Participate in programmes or boot camps designed for career changers.
- ❖ Get guidance from career counsellors or coaches.
- ❖ Attend job fairs and networking events in your new field.

3. Explore Entry-Level Roles:

- ❖ Apply for entry-level positions in a new industry.
- ❖ Highlight transferable skills from your previous career.
- ❖ Embrace the chance to start fresh and work your way up.

Altruistic Endeavours

1. **Contribute to the Non-Profit Sector:**
   - ❖ Work for non-profit organisations or charities that align with your values.
   - ❖ Utilise your skills to support causes you're passionate about.
   - ❖ Seek roles in administration, fundraising or outreach programmes.

2. **Volunteer Your Time:**
   - ❖ Take part in community service projects or international missions.
   - ❖ Provide pro-bono services in your area of expertise to non-profits.
   - ❖ Get involved in local community initiatives or support groups.

3. **Offer Mentorship:**
   - ❖ Mentor younger professionals or students.
   - ❖ Join mentorship programmes through professional associations.
   - ❖ Share your knowledge and experience to help others grow.

Mentioned below are some of the niches and skills you can venture out and explore. These are a few which are most common. You can create an idea, a business or skill unique to you.

1. Freelance Writing: Offer writing services for blogs, websites or magazines.

2. Virtual Assistant: Provide administrative support to businesses remotely.

3. Online Tutoring: Teach subjects you are passionate about through online platforms.

4. Social Media Manager: Manage social media accounts for businesses or influencers.

5. Graphic Design: Offer design services for logos, websites or marketing materials.

6. Content Creation: Develop content for social media, websites or marketing campaigns.

7. Fitness Instructor: Teach fitness classes or offer personal training sessions.

8. Photography: Start a photography business for events, portraits or products.

9. Life Coaching: Help others achieve their personal or professional goals.

10. Consulting: Provide expertise in your previous professional field.

11. Translation Services: Offer translation services if you are bilingual or multilingual.

12. Holistic Healing: Become a certified practitioner in fields like yoga, acupuncture or massage therapy.

13. Voice Acting: Provide voiceover work for audiobooks, commercials or animations.

14. Event Planning: Plan and organise events such as weddings, parties or corporate functions.

15. Interior Design: Offer home decorating and design services.

16. Cooking/Baking Classes: Teach cooking or baking classes in person or online.

17. Writing a Book: Write and publish a book, either fiction or non-fiction.

18. Home Organisation: Help people declutter and organise their homes.

19. Public Speaking: Become a motivational speaker or offer workshops and seminars.

20. Blogging/Vlogging: Start a blog or YouTube channel about a topic you love.

21. E-commerce Store: Sell products online via platforms like Etsy, Amazon or Shopify.

22. Crafts and Handmade Goods: Create and sell handmade items like jewellery, candles or clothing.

23. Real Estate Agent: Get licensed and help people buy or sell properties.

24. Non-profit Work: Join or start a non-profit organisation for a cause you care about.

25. Personal Shopper/Stylist: Help people with their fashion and shopping needs.

26. Gardening/Landscaping: Start a gardening or landscaping business.

27. Pet Sitting/Dog Walking: Offer pet care services in your local area.

28. Travel Planning: Create and sell travel itineraries or become a travel consultant.

29. Art and Painting: Create and sell your artwork or offer art classes.

30. App Development: Develop apps or websites if you have a background in tech.

b. The Yearn to Learn and Earn Beyond Academics, Through the School of Life

In other words, I wove my hopes and dreams,

Through struggles, doubts and silent screams.

Each step a lesson, each fall a guide,

Resilience born from deep inside.

Beyond the books, life's lessons gleam,

A journey lived, a writer's dream.

Learning beyond formal education is about embracing curiosity and maintaining a lifelong desire for growth. It's about seeking knowledge in everyday interactions, observing the world with an open mind, and being willing to adapt and evolve.

Whether it's through travel, reading, engaging in meaningful conversations or simply reflecting on personal experiences, every encounter enriches our understanding of life.

Writing this book was one such exploration. It has been a deeply personal and transformative journey, not just for me but for the countless women whose lives I've had the privilege to touch. Every page is imbued with the raw honesty of my experiences, the hard-earned wisdom I've gained, and the mistakes that have shaped me. Sharing my knowledge has been a labour of love, an act of vulnerability that has allowed me to connect with others on a profound level.

The yearning to change lives has been my guiding light, propelling me forward even in the face of uncertainty. There were moments of doubt and times when I questioned my path, but each challenge taught me the invaluable lesson of resilience. These struggles were not setbacks but stepping stones, each one reinforcing my belief in the power of perseverance.

Recognition has been both a humbling and surreal experience. It's a reminder that our efforts, no matter how small they may seem, can have far-reaching impacts. Yet, it is gratitude that keeps me firmly grounded. I am thankful for every story shared, every life touched and every woman who has found strength in her struggles through my words. This sense of gratitude fuels my passion for mentoring and supporting women, particularly those seeking to reverse health disorders and reclaim their lives again in career. *The greatest challenges we face are not the ones imposed by the world around us, but those that lie within. It's the internal battles, the silent struggles with self-doubt and fear, that often hold us back. By confronting and overcoming these inner obstacles, we unlock the potential to achieve greatness and inspire others to do the same.*

 # SUMMARY

Default – Direction- Design

As you turn the final pages of this book, I hope you've felt the heartbeat of every story, the pulse of every struggle, and the triumph of every victory. This journey has been more than just words on a page—it rekindles the indomitable spirit within each of us. Here, in this closing chapter, let's reflect on the path from inhibitions to success, celebrating the freedom found along the way. Starting from a place of uncertainty and drifting through life's defaults, you embark on a transformative journey towards clarity and purpose. This journey signifies an energy shift—from hesitation and ambiguity to intentional direction and empowerment. Each stride forward represents a deliberate choice to reclaim your identity and pursue your passions with renewed determination. Through resilience and self-discovery, you redefine your careers after a break towards a path that honours your aspirations and harnesses your strengths.

Success is not final, failure is not fatal: It is the courage to continue that counts. – Winston Churchill

It's all about accepting ourselves, finding strength in our challenges, and never losing sight of the possibility of a brighter tomorrow that makes us who we are. This journey we've shared through these pages has been about more than just stories; it's been a heartfelt reminder that we are all perfectly imperfect. Remember, the path to freedom is not a solitary journey but a shared experience. Together, we can overcome any challenge that comes our way.

As we part ways, keep this in mind: your journey is uniquely yours, shaped by every experience, every challenge and every triumph. Each detour and stumble have contributed to your incredible resilience. May this book serve not just as a reminder of your strength but as a hand-holding guide to unlocking your fullest potential.

And let's not forget to laugh along the way. Life's too short to take ourselves too seriously. Have you ever confidently sent a message to the wrong group chat, only to realise your mistake when the responses started pouring in?

. Embrace the quirks, the flubs, the moments of sheer brilliance, and the days you trip over your own feet. So, keep dreaming, keep striving and let your spirit soar.

"In the silence of self-doubt, a whisper grows loud, A seed of belief, breaking free from the shroud. With every step forward, fears fade and disperse, Unleashing the power of a life unrehearsed."

Section 4

Workout Worksheet

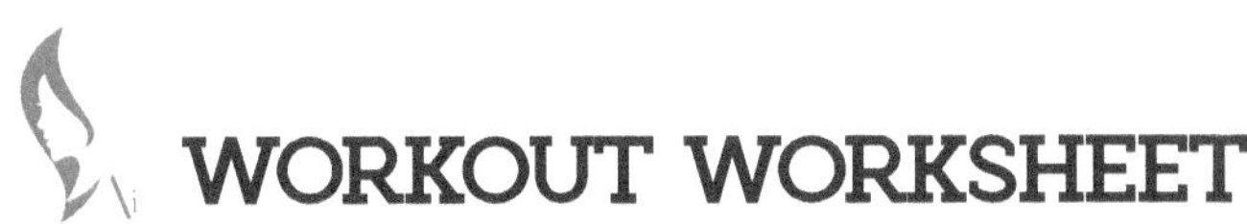

WORKOUT WORKSHEET

Now that you have come this far with me, this section is more of self analysis and reflection. Some of the answer to the prompts below will lead you to gain confidence in yourself. try and make an effort to answer these honestly.

Beyond this page is a page on mindmap. create your small goals and take action on what excites you most.

1. What specific fears do I have about re-entering the workforce while managing family responsibilities, and how might these fears impact my job search and career choices?

2. Which aspects of my professional skills or experience am I most concerned about due to my career break, and what steps can I take to address these concerns and build confidence?

3. Have there been any ways in which my career break or family responsibilities have affected others in my professional or personal circle, and how have I worked to resolve these issues?

4. What are my deepest insecurities about balancing career ambitions with family life, and how do these insecurities affect my self-esteem and professional interactions?

5. What are my major regrets related to the balance between my career and family, and how have these regrets influenced my current professional goals and aspirations?

6. How do I respond to criticism or feedback about my career performance, especially in the context of managing family duties, and what does this reveal about my readiness to adapt and improve?

7. What significant untruths have I told myself or others about my career break or family responsibilities, and what were the underlying reasons for these misconceptions?

8. How do I cope with feelings of inadequacy or failure related to my career and family balance, and are these coping strategies helping or hindering my progress?

9. What are my core professional and personal goals now, and what fears or excuses related to family responsibilities might be holding me back from pursuing them?

10. In what ways do I seek validation from others about my ability to manage both career and family, and how does this impact my self-worth and decision-making?

MIND MAPS FOR GOAL PLANNING

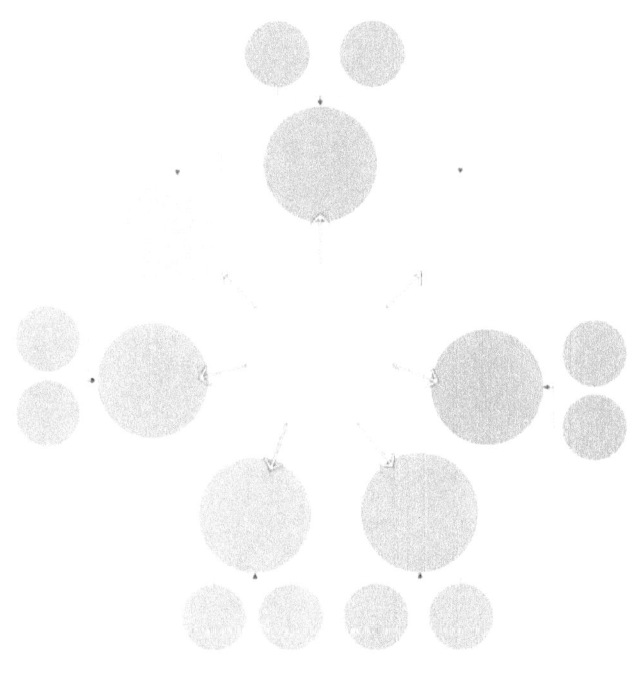

I
am
Abundant

NEVER
GIVE UP
ON YOUR
DREAMS

DON'T
STOP
until
you're
PROUD